Until You Sleep In My Bed

Jacqueline Childs-Taliaferro

Until You Sleep In My Bed

Copyright © 2022 Jacqueline Childs-Taliaferro

ISBN Printbook: 9781675646632

All rights reserved.

Unless otherwise indicated, all scripture, quotations are taken from the King James Version of the Bible.

Shekinah Glory
PUBLISHING

www.shekinahglorypublishing.org

(936) 314-7458

Acknowledgments

I thank the Holy Spirit for enlightening me with divine ideas and anointing every word in this book. I thank my husband Luke, my champion, for his prayers, consistent support, and encouragement. I thank my publisher for her expertise. Finally, I thank my family for believing in me and loving me to be all I can be.

Table of Contents

Until You Sleep In My Bed

BETWEEN THE LINES

Not knowing what life is all about, just trying hard to
figure It out.
Got to read between the lines, the world has
changed–difficult times.
You look at me as if I've got it going on.
Good job, living life on the upswing, but for me, it's
all wrong.
Living paycheck to paycheck, credit cards maxed out,
and life is a wreck.
Wouldn't listen to a soul. This is my life. I know how
to roll.
Depression hits me up and down,
I smile a lot to hide the frown.
I pray, but I don't think He hears me.
Have never been one to believe, just so tired of being
deceived.
Until you sleep in my bed, you can't get in my head.

Until You Sleep In My Bed

FAITH THAT IS SHAKEN

"Without faith, it is impossible to please God!"

A lack of faith tells God you don't believe He can help you nor bring you out of a grueling situation. This could mean your faith has been shaken, and I know exactly how that feels.

I recall a time when I was about six years old. After playing outside in the hot sun with my friends, I ran into the house to get a drink of water. Because I was unable to reach the sink on my own, I grabbed the step stool and proceeded to climb up to the fountain over the sink to get a drink of water. Next to the sink, my mother was preparing a pot of food on the stove. I remember the breeze coming through the side door into the kitchen, making the flames under the pot dance a little. However, I did not notice that the flames had danced their way unto me until I ran back outside to rejoin my friends, and they yelled, "Your dress is on fire!"

I did not immediately feel the flames on my body, but once I did, I ran back into the house, yelling and screaming to my mother for help. My father was at work, so one of the neighbors drove my mother and me quickly to the hospital. My mother began to peel the hot, burned skin from my severely burned back during the ride causing second-degree burns to my mother's hands. While I was in The Children's hospital for months, I witnessed many children who were so sick. There was a boy without a neck, just his hand and shoulders. Another child there was born without legs, and another who had injured himself from jumping over a barbed wire fence running from a wild dog—seeing these things frightened me greatly, and at an early age, that was my beginning of faith that can be shaken.

So many Christians have left the church because the preacher has been caught up in a scandal, which means their faith was in the preacher and not in God. In 1st Kings 18:21, it speaks of the chief god of the Canaanites, whose name was Ba'al. When Elijah came to the people and warned them of Ba'al, he said, "How long will you waver between two opinions? If God be God, follow him; but if Ba'al, then follow him." Sometimes you must stand alone in your faith, be still, and follow your faith in God and what you believe He and only He can do for you.

Some people have a wounded spirit. After years of being faithful servants and dedicated pillars in the church, someone has disrespected them with slander, and they leave, vowing never to enter the doors of a sanctuary again. Their faith was shaken. What turmoil in your life experience has shaken your faith? Have you come to that place within yourself where it is time to dive deeper into God, into that God-like faith? In addition, you must give up the sickness that is worrying you, that fear, doubt, and disbelief of looking for someone else to make you happy. Give up the faith in your business that you are the only one that can make it work. Give up that dependence upon alcohol, drugs, gambling, or the insatiable drive to be validated by everyone.

Let your faith in God lead you into a deeper dependence on God and not be shaken by your own dependencies. Need a word? Look at Luke 22:31-32, "And the Lord said, Simon, Simon, behold satan has desired to have you, that he may sift you
3.2as wheat, but I prayed for you that your faith would not fail and when you are converted reach back and strengthen your brother or sister."

Has your faith been shaken to the point of no return when you lost a loved one to violence, and you cannot forgive the one who took their life? Has your faith been shaken when the diagnosis from the doctor implied that the threat of a terminal disease has returned? Are you shaken to the point of questioning God, "Why me?" Reach into yourself, pull out the faith God gave you before tragedy hit your life, and say I will not give in to doubt or fear. I will fight the good fight of faith. I will live and make it through. My faith is a God-given faith. Though my faith may be shaken from time to time because of life's perils, my faith is in God, and He will never leave me nor forsake me.

Until You Sleep In My Bed

REJECTION

The rejection you feel when looked over for the promotion.

The time invested in education after the pursuit of three degrees and told you are an overachiever, as they hope you get discouraged and leave.

Oh no, I will not be compromised.

I will leave on my terms and on my time.

Tired when evening comes at home as I doze off in bed,
the bedroom door opens slightly at three o'clock in the morning to see if I'm sleeping because you just got in from a midnight creep.

Until you sleep in my bed, you can't get in my head.

Until You Sleep In My Bed

SOMETIMES GOD WILL SEND YOU BACK

Sometimes God will send you back to a place of suffering for the next phase of your life to build you into a tower of strength to avoid turning into a pillar of salt. Ask God to help you understand that this place is not to cause you harm, even if it may feel like it, but to be of great help.

There are some lessons that you need to learn. Some issues that you need to let go of or some things that need to be worked out in you. Before God can place you in the right place, you must get in the right position. He wants to open new doors, show you new opportunities in this season, and do away with the former things, so stop resisting God. You may think you know it all, but you don't. Humble yourself and allow God to do what He needs to do.

Endure the process and know that the rewards are for your good. God's favor is upon you, and the outcome will fill you with substance that will grow with you from level to level. No more feeling that you've got it going on. Only He does!

Until You Sleep In My Bed

A DESIRE

As I continue to pursue my education, my goal is to research a cure for dementia and Alzheimer's.

Trying not to apply for any student loans, instead, buy books and avoid the expense of keeping a phone.

My mainstream income between studies—I'm known as "Sugar." I slide up and down a poll quite physically fit and not that ole.

There are so many times I come home without sleep, must study for classes and not let discouragement creep.

The smell of smoke and drunken men from the club lingers,
I don't feel ashamed of what I do.

I have a desire to make life better for others to pursue.
Until you sleep in my bed, you can't get in my head.

Until You Sleep In My Bed

PRAYER FOR GUIDANCE

Lord, you see and know all things.
Uncover and reveal to me that I may see and know
as you do.

What are you trying to show me?
Don't let me be deceived, don't let me be a fool.

Keep me paying attention.
What are you trying to tell me?

What do I need to know?
Show me the way, Lord, take my hand and help me
to follow your direction.

Delight my ears that it is only your voice I hear.
Cleanse my spirit to be obedient to your way.

Purge me of my ways and replace me with more of
You so I will know Your word and keep it in my
heart.

I pray this prayer in Jesus' name,
Amen.

Until You Sleep In My Bed

HAVE I LOST MY DIRECTION?

Does life seem to be passing me by?
Should I throw in the towel?
Is it me, or is it the circumstances surrounding me?
I pray but receive no answer.
I feel as if I am just existing and serving no purpose.
Is there really a God?
Am I just gonna go through life with this void?
There was a time in my life when I felt needed, a time when things were less complicated—a time when I would burst out in laughter for no reason at all.
Is there really a God that hears my cry that sees the tears when they fall from my eyes.
How can I find myself when I feel I have lost my direction?
Where is the love I once had?
Why am I full of such despair?
Have I sunk so low?
I have sunk beyond the bottom that if I can just pull myself up and get to the bottom, then maybe I will find hope to make it to the top.
When I pray, is my heart filled with such bitterness, remorse, unforgiveness, or jealousy that God just does not hear me?
Where did I go wrong?
I am such a good person. What happened to me?

Is it me, or is it them?
So many questions wander through my mind.
I feel so conflicted. Lord, hear my cry.
Am I so full of myself that I can't hear you?
Lord, have you forgotten me? Are you there?
How can I get back to you?

Isaiah 49:15 says, "See! I will not forget you. I have carved you on the palm of my hand."

Until You Sleep In My Bed

DEAR LORD JESUS

2 Timothy 3:2 speaks of the "Evil Last Days." The scripture says, "In the last days terrible times will come, for men will be lovers of themselves, lovers of money, boastful, disobedient, ungrateful and unholy, unloving, unforgiving, slanderous, without self-control, headstrong, haughty, lovers of pleasures rather than lovers of God, having a form of godliness but denying it's power and from such people turn away. For of this sort are those who creep into households and make capture of gullible silly women loaded down with sins, led away by various lust. Always learning and never able to come to the knowledge of the truth. They resist the truth, but they will progress no further, for their folly will come to an end."

Oh Lord, this is what I face, and it gives me understanding through your word. Oh Jesus, where do I go from here? I need your guidance and your direction. I don't want to go alone, and I don't want to lean to my own understanding and go on my own. I must trust you with all my heart and seek your face, and you will direct my path. If I go on my own, I go blindly, but if I wait and trust you to guide me, I believe you will work it out for me. I feel a spirit of rejection and abandonment; however, I don't want to do something against your will. Lord, only you hold my future in your hand.

Lord, heal my mind. Give me peace down on the inside. Remove any anxiety. Give me a life of contentment and peace. Remove any unforgiveness and bitterness. Help me to love the unlovely in my life. Deliver me and set me free mentally, physically, morally, and financially. Help me see your blessings in my life and not the ugly situation I face.

Psalm 50:15 states, "CALL UPON ME IN THE DAY OF YOUR TROUBLE, I SHALL STRENGTHEN YOU AND YOU WILL GLORIFY ME." Lord, I am calling upon you to heal my emotions. Remove the spirit of being left out or deserted. Forgive me, Lord, if I have any resentment, hate, any evil thoughts, or lack of faith. Help me to speak words of kindness instead of a spiteful tongue. Jesus, let my life be filled with your joy that I may look beyond the faults of others.

It is hard for me to be kind-spirited during these aging years. Please give me a life filled with your presence near me. Fill my life with the comfort of the Holy Spirit. Remove any fear, doubt, or disbelief. Help me to pray and believe that "prayer changes things."

Deliver me and set me free from any lonesomeness and help me to depend on you to see me through. Job

14:14 reads, "ALL THE DAYS OF MY TROUBLE I WILL WAIT UNTIL MY CHANGE COMES."
Help me, Jesus, pray for others, hold on, and give me the tolerance I need just to ride it out and let God bring it to an end.

In Jesus' name, I pray,
AMEN.

Until You Sleep In My Bed

JUST BECAUSE

Just because I never told you I needed you didn't mean I was strong.

Just because it never rained on your side of the street, it stormed on mine.

I gave you up for adoption and never looked back. At least I didn't raise you in the jungle-infested life I live in.

Just because you can't forgive me doesn't mean I've given up hope.

Locked up in a world of my own doesn't give you the right to judge me just because.

Until you sleep in my bed, you can't get in my head!

Until You Sleep In My Bed

A MOTHERLESS CHILD

Mother died, and father couldn't be a father anymore, so he walked away.

Oh, how I cried!

Separated from my sibling severely mistreated in foster homes.

Felt so alone.

Not even fourteen years of age needed to survive started stealing cars to sleep in, pregnant with child.

Oh, how I cried.

I'm twenty-five, the mother of four, working three jobs.

But now, when I wipe a tear, I do not live in fear because I'm alive. My children are beautiful, and I am still here.

Until you sleep in my bed, you can't get in my head.

Until You Sleep In My Bed

WHAT BROKE YOU?

What caused you to give up or let time cheat you from making it over to the other side? Was it spiritual, mental, physical, financial, or everyday living? Was it your mother, a woman or man? The heart can be deceitful; therefore, you need to temper your heart.

What is in your heart? You must get beyond yourself so that you can live again. Every time you try and get up, that same botheration comes to pull you, to toss you, to drive you to the brink. The memory of your mother who abandoned you; the one who told you— "You look like your daddy." The one who lived a life of embarrassment when company would come over. The one who would entertain men when she thought you were asleep. The back door opened and closed all night, and you could hear the foot traffic.

Moreover, what kept you sinking from time to time? Was it a financial dilemma, the casino, your choice of drug, or that insatiable desire that you will not be outdone? That drive that keeps you trying to outdo, out dress, outmaneuver, out steal, out cheat, out manipulate, out-sing, or out-compete. What keeps you from getting back up again?

What broke you? Was it the loss of a son or daughter in a tragic accident? Every year on their birthday, you slip into a dark place and must fight to pull yourself back up again. Was it the divorce of your mother and your father? Did your mother get remarried and raised another family, but you and your siblings were forgotten? Or was it when you had to spend one week with your mother and one week with your dad, and you felt pulled and torn between two different lifestyles, and your identity was compromised? Or was it because your parents remarried other people and you had to share your life with an extended family of step-siblings that you never connected with.

Have you been holding it against someone all these years, and it has left you with trust issues? You don't know the whole story, and someone won't tell you the entire truth, anything but the truth. What broke you? Was it that foster home you grew up in because someone decided to abandon you or place you in the adoption system? Was it the foster parents who took you in for profit and not for love?

Furthermore, was it being an only child watching your mother or father choose another man or woman over you? Have you deprived yourself of having a relationship with a family member because something went wrong years ago? Were you broken into pieces and didn't know you were broken until later in life, and you resented your past because you felt you lost so much time that you couldn't make up? What broke you?

Regarding this matter, here is something that may help: I call it hateration when people condescend. You begin to feel good about yourself, take the high road, and love the God in you. When they cackle, you tackle. Tackle with the spirit of love and kindness. Let your light so shine that others may see and know your redeemer lives and lives big within you.

When they hate, you create. Create with forgiveness. You have to forget the things behind you and press toward the light of a higher calling in Christ Jesus. When they try to kill your spirit—you heal! When they steal your joy and destroy your positive attitude, let the spirit of God lift you into a place of healing your mind, body, and soul. You may be broken, but you are blessed.

Genesis 32:24-30 iterates that God must break us from our self-dependence so that He can bless us as we cling to Him in our brokenness. Brokenness is the path to blessing. Before God can use a person greatly, He must break them because we have a built-in propensity to trust in ourselves before trusting in God. Let God put you back together. You aren't broke. You are just bent a little.

Until You Sleep In My Bed

A CALL TO MOTHERS WITH SONS

To all you mothers out there, this is some good sound teaching to all who are willing to be "obedient" to hear the wisdom of experience. So many mothers do not know when to stop preaching and start praying. As a mother, it's challenging to let go and let God have His way and know when to cut the umbilical cord to let a young man grow up and rest in the morals of what he was taught. As a mother, it's difficult to trust that your son must stumble and fall, so you can pray and ask the Lord to pick him up.

Factually, a mother doesn't realize stumbling blocks are the building blocks for their future. How did you make it through the storms of life? How were you able to get back up? How are you making it each time you fall?

A mother also fails to realize that her son is NOT your husband, and even when you get a husband or if you have one, you cannot make your husband your son. A husband has already become a man. A son is still trying to become a man, and the only way he can get there is alone. Some mothers don't realize that when a son enters into his twenties, the mother has to stop preaching and get him there by praying.

Also, if you are still preaching, ask God to deliver that preaching spirit out of you and grace you with a praying spirit for your son. If you are married and still preaching to your husband, ask God to give you a praying spirit for that man. Sit back and quietly watch the hand of God move. Some mothers feel their son is not mature, but they don't realize that maturity comes with growth and time. Preaching after a while goes in one ear and out the other. Praying goes to the soul.

Teaching...
"If you would have your son to walk honorably through the world, you must not attempt to clear the stones from his path but teach him to walk firmly over them - not insist upon leading him by the hand, but let him learn to go alone."

Until You Sleep In My Bed

RELATIONSHIP 101 AS A PARENT

Disconnected from your children? Are you yearning for a relationship with them and wanting to meet their approval? Sometimes, we must listen and be less of a dictator as a parent. Listening to their thoughts will tell you a lot about where they are, regardless of their age. Pray and ask God for His divine guidance when you seem to hit a brick wall and don't have the answer. Praying will help you wait and get in tune with your inner being, the Holy Spirit. He will help you wait, bridle your tongue, and let God step in.

For instance, when my son was 19 years of age, he decided to move out. Although I knew he was a very sound young man, it rocked me. As his mother, I raised him to be independent and flap his wings, but I knew he was not ready to fly alone. For one year, I fasted and prayed and stayed at the foot of Jesus. I was totally dedicated to seeking God. I knew my son had not chosen a world of vice. He just wanted his independence and his own apartment.

I stayed in prayer and read the word of God. After a year, God brought my son home, and he said to me, "Ma, I thought you would be glad I am home." I let my son know I was happy he was home, but I also knew he needed that experience. Two years later, his wings were fully developed, and he independently moved to embrace a life of his own and continued his college education.

There are times when only prayer, staying in the word and letting God step in, that you will gain the help you need to stand fast, be immoveable ever abounding in the work and word of the lord. In those times, God will strengthen a relationship. In those times, the Holy Spirit will let you know what to say when to say it, and how. Or sometimes, as my mother used to say, "Silence is golden."

I have a very dear person in my life who has a disconnected relationship with her mother and, through the years, needed the advice and support only a mother could give. For ten years, she endured many health and life experiences alone. She had a colon removed because of polys attached to her colon, and while under anesthesia, she flatlined, but God brought her out.

She told me afterward she had to have surgery again, but this time a complete hysterectomy. Then there was a hernia repair where she developed a blood clot on the lung, but again, God brought her through. Later a gall bladder had to be removed, and then orthopedic surgery on both feet for heel spurs and just recently back surgery where she was told she could become crippled permanently.

Within 30 days, she lost two sisters and a sister-in-law. She shared with me initially that she did not have a relationship with God and had stopped going to church, but after she flatlined, she developed a relationship with God. Every time she had surgery, God pulled her out each time, and now, she feels confident about herself.

Conclusively, she has since then been delivered from holding on to bitterness toward her mother, and that relationship has gotten better. She has a total life change. She says God gave her a second chance by blessing her with a church home she prayed for. God is a God of so many possibilities. He took a chance on us when we were born.

Until You Sleep In My Bed

THE BRIDGE

During the day, I escape looking out over the water under a bridge, being stared at as others drive by, wondering if I am high.

Resting over rocks that comfort me.
At night in a vacant building is where I sleep.

My bed is the hard one, with no pillows or sheets.
A cardboard slate, but for me, not so great.
I've become accustomed to the stench that reeks.

Today I found a mattress in an alley that is nice and soft, even if it's filled with the slump of someone's body.

Watching my friends, the roaches, on a wall and mice big and tall. My life seems like a bottomless hole filled with negative thoughts and nightmares of a hopeless soul homeless, no skills as I continue to grow old.

Until you sleep in my bed, you can't get in my head.

Until You Sleep In My Bed

A SECOND CHANCE

A second chance was given to you, a chance to make life brand new, a way out of the drugs, an escape from a life of bad choices and thugs.

You didn't know you were too weak to handle the challenge. You continued to welcome other addicts into your new world with a kind heart until your life you couldn't manage.

A second chance at the sweet lady's home she let you rent became commonplace for others without your consent.

You live now on a roller coaster of dreams, entertained by the drug dealers, addicts, and alcoholics as you listen while they communicate about their fraudulent schemes.

A second chance again seems so far away because you've been evicted with no place to stay.

Homeless just like your friends, trying to find shelter but don't know when this kind of living will end.
Until you sleep in my bed, you can't get in my head.

Until You Sleep In My Bed

PRAYER OF SALVATION

Dear Lord,

Save me, sanctify me, and fill me with the infilling of the Holy Spirit, deliver me, and set me free. Free me mentally, physically, morally, spiritually, and financially.

Lord, I want to be free, whole, and complete. I desire to serve you and let my light so shine through me so that others may see your glory living in me.

Help me to trust you with all my heart and lean not to my own understanding, acknowledge you in all my ways, and allow you to direct my path. Lord, show me the way and let your truth live big in me.

In Jesus' name,
Amen

Until You Sleep In My Bed

A WILDERNESS

There's a place of fear, doubt, and disbelief, and it's called a wilderness. A wilderness is where we feel bound to something that has happened to us. What is it that is so deeply lodged in you, that keeps you bound and keeps you from moving forward?

Is it unforgiveness? Who did what? Who said what? Every time you think you've gotten past trauma, the bad memory pulls you back. The Lord says, "Come follow me!" But how can I get past my past to follow? The seed of offense planted inside you years ago took root and grew into a root of bitterness, unforgiveness, and low self-esteem. That small thing grew into a big thing, and it pushed love out the way. The situation repetitiously clouds your thinking.

Examples in the word we should look at were when Paul said, "Oh, I go to do good, but evil is ever-present." Job said, "When I try and seek God, I go to my left, but I can't find him. I go to my right, but sometimes he is not there though I am tested yet will I trust him." I will trust the Lord no matter what and no matter how many times I fall. Jacob had a thorn in his side, something that troubled him deeply, but he was determined to get past it, so he wrestled with *his faith and told the Lord, "I am not going to move until you bless me." I am reminded of the five porches in the bible and how one man sat on the porch crippled by the things of life for 38 years before his faith became so strong one day he got up and walked off into a new life.*

Sometimes it takes years for us to come out of ourselves and go all the way into God, years to walk out of ourselves and live in the newness of life our God has prepared for us. The life just to be free with less turmoil where the enemy does not use anything to harm you or disappointments to torment you. When we can say to ourselves, I'm determined to live drama free and detach myself from other people's empty talk, which pulls me into their dilemma/drama. I love them, but I cannot continue to be them. I must wrestle my way out with faith. Who did this to you? Why did you allow it to control you? Above all, God sees everything, including your emptiness.

Trust God with your bitterness, unforgiveness, your wayward son or daughter, grandchild, husband, sister or brother, the man you just can't pull away from, cancer, arthritis, your bad knees, diabetes, and heart problem. Just trust the God in you to bring you out of the wilderness and live life, love yourself to the fullest, and love life. When you trust the God in you, you can begin to live more abundantly because God lives big in you.

Until You Sleep In My Bed

LORD, YOU SPARED ME

When the doctor told you, you had stage three cancer, and you've been walking around living a life for the past several years or so, know that the Lord spared you. When your home was targeted in the neighborhood as the house of many pleasures because of your mother's indiscretions, the Lord spared you and made sure you did not follow in her footsteps. He spared you when that woman solicited your daughter, and later your boyfriend violated her. You thought you would lose your mind at times, but He spared you. You can't get past the foster care system and how you were left behind, but He has spared you. He took you into His fold and surrounded you with loving people and friendships.

When you thought you couldn't make it that time, your husband abandoned you and chose to live separately and raise another woman's children. God spared you, helped you pick up the pieces, and kept you forging ahead. The Lord spared you time and time again when you were trying to make ends meet financially. You were up one day down the next, and He spared you. You've attended countless weddings but have never been married. When you've witnessed the married couples divorcing, you realize God spared you. You've had an abortion, but He allowed you to have more children afterward and spared you. Your brother and mother are on drugs, but the Lord spared you. Never had a desire to drink or smoke. Chained for years to a thought of having someone you couldn't have, God, spared and delivered your mind from those thoughts.

The bible tells us this:
The Lord God is a sun and shield He protects. He gives grace and glory, and no good thing shall He withhold from those who walk upright before Him.

Let us pray:

Lord, I give myself to you. I give up everything that has held me bound because you have spared me. I could have been gone, but you held on to me, and you spared my life. Lord, thank you for sparing me, thank you for not giving up on me when I gave up on myself. Lord, thank you for saving me. Lord, you spared me, and for this, I thank you.

In the name of Jesus,
Amen.

Until You Sleep In My Bed

I'M TRYING TO FORGIVE, BUT I CAN'T!

If I don't forgive you, I am allowing you to keep holding me back. I may not like you, but I must forgive you because my blessings will not be blocked if I forgive you. No matter what we do in life, how we do it, why or when we do it, does not matter to God because our Lord Jesus Christ is a forgiving God. He sees all, knows all, and is a God of second chances. If the Lord gives us a second chance, we must forgive others and give them a second chance.

Who have you allowed to plague your life? They may be dead and gone, and you are still holding on. What happened to you that you just cannot forgive yourself or forgive them?

People are our experiences for growth. When you can learn to forgive, you can learn to love unconditionally. I reminisce about a beautiful person I had known from when her sister was just a young girl. She said there has always been a distance between them, like Esau and Jacob or Cain and Abel, who were brothers during the bible days.

She would tell me how much she yearned for her younger sisters' affections, but her sister was full of spite, jealousy, dislike, and rage. This kept this beautiful person with deep concern that led to health challenges knowing she had not wronged her in any way.

The other day I had an opportunity to call the older sister. She gave such a wonderful testimony regarding how after 60 years of torment, she found forgiveness in her heart for her younger sister and how free she is, and her love for her. Her sister is still the same, but God brought deliverance to her because she could let go and forgive. God can do anything but fail.

We think, why does it take so long for God to move a stumbling block? Could it be that we are not waiting for God, but God is waiting for us to ask Him to help us let go? The Lord has brought so many of us through in our lives with the gift of forgiveness. Forgiveness turns hate into love, and love helps us see both sides of reality.

Matthew 5:44 reads, "But I say unto you, love your enemies, bless them that curse you, do good to them that hate you and pray for them which despitefully use you, and persecute you."

God has given this beautiful person a second chance to live out her later years in peace with her sister's rejection against her. Forgiveness is another tool to help us overcome the tragedies and misfortunes we experience through life's learned lessons.

For example, many say, "I can forgive, but I won't forget." When forgiveness comes from deep within the heart, the memory of the offense introduces a truth so real that we actually have peace that surpasses all human understanding.

God is a God of second chances. He gives us a chance to get it right, a chance to heal to a place where we can stand and say, yes, that happened, but it really doesn't matter to me anymore! God has fixed my heart; my mind has been regulated to a healing place of peace. No matter what the story is in your life, let your story summary be– God has fixed my heart, and my mind has been regulated to a healing place of peace.

Matthew 6:15 reads, "But if you do not forgive others their sins, your Father will not forgive your sins."

I read somewhere that the wealthiest places on earth are not the oil fields of the middle east or the diamond mines in South Africa. The wealthiest places are the cemeteries. Buried in the ground are never formed businesses, songs that were never sung, books that were never written, potential never realized, dreams that never came to pass, and unforgiveness never released.

Good morning...
Good morning unforgiveness. You know I must let you go. Good evening pain and suffering; you are no longer welcome here. Good night arthritis: you no

longer live in my body due to the past. I forgive you, why? Because I didn't know I was holding on to anything. How did I find out? My body told me through the highs and lows of depression and the immune response. It was not just grief. It was not letting go of regret, among other things.

Today I must begin a new life as I sit down and drink a cup of peace. I don't feel new, but I feel loved. I let go of sympathy, and I welcome forgiveness. I welcome a conscious decision to let go of worry, doubt, disbelief, and any past regrets.

I know this, too, will pass because I deserve to live. I will continue to honor the God in me that helps me get up each morning and say thank you, Lord. I let go of any crutches that are holding me back, and I embrace the faith of our Lord Jesus Christ that is holding me up.

Most importantly, I live because God lives in me. I forgive myself for holding on to anything unhealthy, and I forgive any regrets. I am grateful for the strength God has given me to let go and let God have his way. Helping me make decisions I need to make. I welcome this new chapter where I walk unafraid. My lease on my past has expired, and I am under a new covenant agreement with God. Good morning new life. I welcome a new day and walk in faith, whether I am hesitant. I am free because time will help me feel free. Forgive not because the person deserves it. Forgive so you can have peace!

Until You Sleep In My Bed

LOOKING FOR LOVE

Love has many faces. Before it surrenders to kindness, the face of jealousy has the face of hope. What are we looking for in love? Do we desire someone to comfort us or be a crutch, validated or fulfilled? What is love? Where can we find it? Just look within and feel the God within.

According to the word and will of God, love is kind, forgiving, and it bears all things. Love weathers the storms of life, which means getting you through those rough places. Love must love the unloving, the person who smiles in our face but scorns us every chance they get. Love is not rude or selfish, and it doesn't always have to have its own way. Go within and find yourself. God is love; therefore, let Him heal the hurt, distrust, and anger that rages within.

Let God remove the years of broken dreams, wipe away the past, and mend a life filled with unforgiveness. The lord says, "If you love me, keep my commandments and love those who despitefully misuse you." Love your enemy-relative who ignores you, held something against you since you were kids, and made a difference between you and the rest of your siblings or cousins.

Since God is love, love has no barriers. It reaches obstacles, goes into the darkest place in our lives, and heals that root of bitterness so deeply lodged. It goes deep within and erases the hurt. Are you looking for someone to love you? Can you love yourself? If you can love yourself, love will find you.

Love is that person after many years who walks into your life and says I was wrong, the one who you forgave and let go of years ago. God is love. He touches the heart, opens it up, and allows it to breathe again. Love heals the mind, and once the mind is healed, the body recovers.

When the mind is free, your life is free. When your life is free, you can face tomorrow without any doubt. When the mind is clear, your thoughts are positive, and you'll no longer waver back and forth. Let God into your heart and heal the very pulse of your existence. Let the hurt roll out of your life into a stream of forgetfulness.

Love is someone's mother who doesn't call and wishes them a happy birthday on the very day. She brought them into this world; however, that person realizes that their mother is the one who is void of love, but they love their mother no matter what and beyond disappointment. Undoubtedly, love also is the one who found within themself to love unconditionally the parent who made a noticeable difference of rejection from the rest of the siblings.

Another great example is a wife who walks away from her family and abandons the children, or a husband abandon's his marriage for another woman or another man. Love steps in, weathers the storm, places itself into survival mode by any means necessary, and the love in that person who's left behind burrows. Through the situation by faith step by step, day by day, beyond rejection, ask the Lord to help them make it through.

Thus love transforms hate, bitterness, and hurt, but one of the greatest rewards in life is letting the Lord transform you from every level of your past to migrate you into the greatest love of God, and that is the gift of your precious life. You are moving forward from so much baggage, so much darkness starting over each time from the death of a loved one, the loss of your home, a marriage gone wrong, a son or daughter making a decision to lead an alternative lifestyle, visiting a penal institution where one of your children's father or mother has been incarcerated for life. Life will either make you move forward or keep you stuck.

Moving forward, some who have been terminated from a job of several years had gotten denied a pension because the company went overseas. The professional whose job was phased out or the rejection and embarrassment of being passed over for a promotion. Where is the love? Watching the courts award grandchildren to an aging woman facing her sixties just when she raised her own and thought a new life of freedom would await her. Where is the love?

Chiefly, love is prayer, and it changes things because it changes you. Prayer rids you of the deception that life had woven its fabric of distrust into your very being when life left you hopeless. Looking for love? It's been there all along. Love comes from a small child who looks at you in a shopping cart at the grocery store with their parent. Love comes as a wave from an unexpected source, a nod from a little ole senior citizen. Love narrates a scripture in our hearts that keeps us with a calming peace.

Last and greatest of all, love by God is His creative way of orchestrating our lives in a melodic motion that we can never conceive.

"Love bears all things, believes all things, hopes all things, and endures all things (I Corinthians 13:7, KJV)." There are three great things about life—faith, hope, and love. You can move a mountain with your faith and have endless hope for tomorrow, but the greatest of the three is love.

Until You Sleep In My Bed

RELATIONSHIP 101 FOR SINGLE WOMEN

When you get with someone, do you know what you are getting? You can't change anyone. Only God can change someone, but you have to know what you are getting because some people don't want to be changed. God gives us all free will. You must accept the flaws in an individual and the perfections. Do you really know what you are getting in a person? Can you stand the test of time by accepting the flaws before the relationship goes into a deeper commitment?

Furthermore, are you willing to let courtship have its place? Real courtship is getting into a place of adjustment. Is he a selfish individual? Is he the kind that will give gifts but not give of himself? I've heard individuals say opposites attract, but some people have the same traits as others. Are you selfish? If he is not the jealous kind, are you? Are you the one that can't let go of certain vices? What will he have to deal with? No one is perfect, but relationships are hard enough without bringing unsightly demons into the scenario of life. Is he the kind that you will allow him to have you and a side-squeezer, or are you the kind to have him and you have a side-squeezer? Bringing this subject into proper perspective is called being lop-sided.

Therefore, you want to be equally yoked. Second Corinthians 6:14-15 says, "Do not be unequally yoked with unbelievers. What partnership has light with darkness?" You may be the church attendee, or he may not be, but he may have the church in his heart and will go with you occasionally. What is he bringing to the table? Galatians 5:22-24 reads, "But the fruit of the spirit is love, joy, peace, patience, kindness, goodness, faithfulness, gentleness, and self-control." This is relationship 101. Who are you? Do you know yourself?

You don't know what you are getting because you may not know who you are. Wonder why it's taking so long? You must find yourself. How do I find myself? Find Jesus! But I already have. When you go all the way into God and give up yourself and the things of the flesh, you go all the way into God. That's when you find God, and in doing so, He helps you find yourself.

It's called a relationship where God leads to a relationship with yourself. When this happens, God will introduce that right person to you. Then you will know what you are looking for because that person will have the flaws and perfections you can tolerate. Fools rush in where wise men dare to tread. Do you know what you are getting in that person? Let time teach you.

Henceforth, relationship 101 teaches you that you must give a person time to show their true self, so you will know what to deal with. It takes time for someone to show who they really are. They may have trust issues because of a failed relationship, and you must allow time to develop that trust in you, time for you to see if this is someone that will complete you. If you are looking for a quick fix, you are not ready for a real relationship. If you are looking for instant love, you are not ready for a relationship because true love grows with time and is nurtured by a relationship.

In second Timothy 3, the word says, "This know also, that in the last days perilous times shall come. Men shall be lovers of themselves, unthankful and unholy without natural affection. Lovers of pleasures more than lovers of God. Having a form of godliness but denying the power thereof from such turn away. For of this sort are those which creep into houses and lead captive silly women laden with sins led away with lust. Ever learning and never able to come to the knowledge of the truth."

A relationship is one of the keys of life. You encounter relationships with your co-workers, neighbors, supervisor, and teachers, which teaches you how to engage with your enemies. Unless you can have a relationship with our Lord Jesus Christ, you will not enjoy relationships with others.

Love your enemies, even if you don't like them. Above all, love yourself. Love the God in you.

Until You Sleep In My Bed

A HUSBAND THAT GOD GIVES

"And the Lord God said: it is not good that the man Should be alone: I will make him a 'help mate' suitable for him (genesis 2:18, KJV)."

A charge from the Lord is to help him meet his goals on his journey so he can come to himself. Why do I have to do this? "A charge I have to keep, oh Lord, to glorify."

When God gives you a project in the form of a husband to fix, to mold, to love, to encourage when you want encouragement, to pamper when you need pampering, to council when you need that support, to pray for when you need prayer, don't wonder or question the project too much, trust God, through it. His amazing grace at the end of the project will become your partner.

Until You Sleep In My Bed

MARRIED BUT DISCONNECTED

Did God do the choosing, or did you? Sometimes what seems so right can be oh so wrong. Two people in a home so divided their conversations are often misinterpreted. Where is the understanding? When God brings two people together, what appears to be so wrong can really be right. Two cannot walk together in agreement, except they are as one. God has to fuse them together. He must knit you like a soft, warm blanket with each other's faults. The faults include his stubbornness with your impatience and his lack of faith with your ambition to serve god.

As time progresses, an adjustment period enters. For some, it lasts for years depending on each individual's acceptance level and willingness to grow with change during the marriage. You can make the adjustment hard or make it easy through prayer, faith, and allowing God to change you. Some marriages stay disconnected to the point that two people grow apart and just tolerate each other, but I'm reminded of a threefold cord. "Two are better than one because they have a good reward for their labor. If one fall's, the other will lift the other one up. Still, woe to one who is alone when they fall for one has not another to help pick them up if two lie together they have heat: but how can one be warm alone. If anyone overpowers against one of them, two shall resist that person, and a threefold cord is not easily broken. A threefold cord is the Holy Spirit, the man and his wife (Ecclesiastes 4:9-12, KJV)."

Chiefly, a cord created by God. With God in control and the center of the marriage, the cord is so tightly woven, unbreakable, and a bond that cannot be severed. A cord so entwined that no situation or person can untangle. A vow sacred, a love that has been knitted through discord. Lord, how do I get there? How can I get past a cord yanked in many directions as you continue to hold and mold us together? Sometimes, Lord, I try and wait because your word in Proverbs 18:22 says, "The man who finds a wife finds a treasure, he finds a good thing."

Finally, the answer comes. Let him find that good thing in you. The kindness, even though you are not a yes person. The willingness to compromise, nature of patience, and the value of bridling your tongue when you really would like to give him a thing or two. What is it about a threefold cord which only God can create? It is a cord that only time can straighten out, a cord strengthened by faith, bonded with tears, tightened by unconditional love twisted through trials, tested by sickness, formed by finances, garnered by goodness, laced with favor, tried by disagreement, tied together with forgiveness. A spiritual cord has the Holy Spirit of God in it, and it's used to keep two people together. It's the still, small voice within that will convict you into an apology even when you know he is wrong.

Likewise, the cord is motivation that keeps your knees bent in prayer and devotion to the commitment when he has spent too much on foolish things. It's the quiet love that lingers beyond an argument, a soul-lifting song that rings within your heart when you are looking for a peaceful haven to reside in after the storm. The cords the smile on your face when you see lipstick pasted on his jaw from one of the church's sisters when she hugged him and has had her eye on him or the one that's always asking you where your husband is she doesn't see him with you. It's the unconditional love and desire to pray for the church sister attempting to commit or has already committed adultery with your mate.

Most of all, the three-fold cord that only God resides in. It is His cord that you must allow in your marriage. It is His cord that can connect two people together. It's the vital, unbreakable bond between you, the Holy Spirit, and your husband. What is it in you that keeps looking at the wrong in each other? Just ask God to show you yourself, and when He does, it will help you look past the faults and see the goodness.

Everyone has potential, and it's the spirit-filled three-fold cord that will pull two people together and keep them together. Allow God to tighten His cord around your marriage. Keep Him in the center, let Him control through prayer, and trust Him to do it.

Lord, I'm not perfect, my marriage is not perfect, but you are the perfect one with the perfect cord to keep us tied together. I give my marriage to You this day, and I trust You to keep us walking together on one accord.

Through Jesus Christ, Amen.

Until You Sleep In My Bed

PUT ON CHRIST

When things all around you seem to fail and the Lord
Jesus Christ appears to be absent, void, and not listening—put on Christ.

Christ Jesus is the anointed one, the most high God who sits high and looks low. When you put on Christ, you wear him daily through the storm when you don't think he hears you.

You wear him with faith and hope. You put on Christ when everything is dark and dismal, when your back is up against the wall, and there is no way out.

You put on Christ when you've lost your way, sickness racks your body, your faith appears to fail you, and when you're loved ones are tired of listening.

Likewise, you put on Christ when your credit has been damaged and life seems to be so unbearable each day is a regret to wake up.

You put on Christ, and you wear him like a warm sweater on a cool fall day. You wear Christ-like an old worn-out shoe that feels too comfortable to throw out.

You put on Christ and wear him like he wore the crown of thorns which tore into the membranes of his very skull. When you're in pain, tired, and feel like giving up, you put on Christ and wear him and think about the welts he felt as the flesh was torn from his body when beaten.

Importantly, you put on Christ when you think all is lost, nowhere to turn, and no one really cares. You wear Christ close to your heart, cover your mind with his blood in times of depression and wonder if he was hit with depression when he hung on the cross.

Put on Christ as you walk in and out of your home, in your travels, and wonder how he felt when he took a long walk along the streets where he was despised, talked about, and ridiculed.

Put on Christ and wonder how he felt when he lost his job after preaching, healing, and teaching because man decided his fate to carry his own cross, which he would die upon.

Put on Christ and let his body be in your body and his blood be in your blood and know he has been where you are and if he laid down his life so you may live, then keep on living to rise again just as he did. If you keep on living sooner or later, there is a brand new life at the end of your suffering. Now that you have done all you can do—Put on Christ.

Until You Sleep In My Bed

THANK YOU FOR SHARING YOUR TEARS

Today you shared your tears with me. You shared an
emotional side of the tender world you live in. The tears that God bottles up and goes into a divine container placed on the altar of Christ for a virtue of healing.

Today you let me in, and you shared something special a suppressed feeling of being alone, a feeling of anxiety, and a feeling that no one knows your story and there is no one you care to share it with.

How much I admire you for your willingness to forge ahead regardless of the inward pain. The strength in which you dig deep down into yourself and try to rise above and reach for another day.

Thank you for sharing your tears with me, and thank you for letting me come into your private world. Having a moment touched me greatly.

Every time I see you, I see God's grace. I see the seat of his mercy upon your life. Every time you cry, God wipes your eyes with healing, so keep crying. Every time you feel depressed, God lifts you up to see a better day.

When you feel alone, he places his angels around you until your strength comes in. Keep looking ahead and keep walking.

Your life has purpose even if you don't see it, because one day your will. You are loved, blessed, beautiful, and strong person created by god.

Until You Sleep In My Bed

BREATHE ON ME

Lord, breathe on that marriage with the disconnect between them. Lord, breathe on their in-laws and keep them well. Lord breathe on all those looking for love, love that believes all things, hopes all things and endures all things. Lord just breathe into the hearts of so many that cannot forgive themselves or others. Breathe your breath of faith that they may have that god-like faith and blind faith to believe you beyond what they cannot see.

Breathe your breath of life into those who believe they have been forgotten because everything they have ever hoped for has dried up. Lord, breathe, just breathe your healing virtue over sickness, loneliness, despair, rejection, and abandonment.

Lord breathe over the high rising cost of health care and finances. Breathe Lord over failing health, joint pain, inflammation in the body, kidneys, heart ailments, arthritis, cancer, diabetes, and blood pressure. Just breathe!

Lord, breathe and take care of the widows and widowers, those who have lost loved ones, and breathe over our children. Lord, breathe over me. Let your breath fill my mind, soul, and spirit. Breathe, dear God, breathe on me and make me whole, let me feel your presence, let me feel your joy, let me be filled with the infilling of your holy spirit.

In Jesus' name,
Amen

Until You Sleep In My Bed

IT COULD BE ME

It could be me standing on the street with a sign in my hand during the blistering cold of the winter or the sweltering heat of the summer. Lord, I thank you.

It could be me whose son or daughter never contacts to say Happy Mother's Day. Lord, I thank you.

It could be me living in a nursing home that no one ever comes to visit. Lord, I thank you.

It could be me living under a bridge being shut out from a homeless shelter because I could not make the deadline. Lord, I thank you.

It could be me being so selfish that I always want them to listen to me whenever anyone calls, and I never want to hear what they have to say. Lord, I thank you.

It could be me whose husband or wife just told them they are leaving for another woman or man after several years of marriage. Lord, I thank you.

It could be me that the doctor has told you only have two weeks to live or a reoccurring terminal condition has come back with a vengeance, but they have the faith to say, "Lord, I thank you."

It could be me whose son or daughter is missing in action in the military. Lord, I thank you.

It could be me who is stricken with a chronic illness, but you have given me the tenacity to hold on to my faith and keep getting up each day. Lord, I thank you.

It could be me living on skid row with a Ph.D. degree all confused and left without friends or family. Lord, I thank you.

It could be me incarcerated for life, facing the electric chair for a crime I did not commit. Lord, I thank you.

It could be me caged in a one-room dwelling void of a window to see out and view the leaves on the trees come alive during spring or view the snow on naked branches during the winter months. Lord, I thank you.

Lord, for all the times I took you for granted, doubted you, was blinded with fear, only wanted to pray when things were going bad, I say thank you because you have never left me, never withdrew your hand from me, nor have you forsaken me.

1 Thessalonians 5:18
In Everything Give Thanks For This Is The Will Of God Jesus Christ Concerning You.

Until You Sleep In My Bed

HEALING SCRIPTURES TO COMFORT THE SOUL

Exodus 23:25
The lord will keep you free from every disease.

Oh lord, how grateful I am that you have delivered me and set me free from every disease.

Jeremiah 17:14
Heal me, o lord, and I shall be healed; save me, and I shall be saved; for thou art my praise.

Every time I hear a choir sing, my heart is filled with praise, my Lord and Savior, Jesus Christ. You have a miraculous way of lifting me up above any situation.

James 5:15
And the prayer of faith shall save the sick, and the Lord shall raise her up; and if she has committed sins, they shall be forgiven.

Oh, master, how committed you are to your word. Your word comforts my soul and gives me peace down on the inside of my spirit.

Matthew 10:1

And when he had called unto (him) his twelve disciples, he gave them "power" against unclean spirits, to cast them out, and to heal all manner of sickness and all manner of disease.

Gracious Savior, only you can commission your angels and give them the power to surround me, protect me from all negative energy, and heal all manner of sickness and disease from me.

Matthew 9:22

But Jesus turned him about, and when he saw Mary, he said, "daughter," Be of good comfort; thy faith hath made thee whole, and Mary was made whole from that hour.

Oh, Jesus, only you know how to call my name with such power to make me whole and complete. No creature on this earth can complete me with such fullness. Your mercy gives me the confidence to hold on as my strength is renewed day by day.

Psalms 103:3

Who forgiveth all thine iniquities; who health all thy diseases.

Dear Father in heaven, I did not realize how the spirit of forgiveness can erase iniquities, and by your grace, your healing virtue removes all diseases. What a mighty God I serve.

Isiah 41:10
Fear thou not; for I am with thee; be not dismayed; for I am thy god. I will strengthen thee; yea, I will help thee; yea, I will uphold thee with the right hand of my righteousness.

Until You Sleep In My Bed

A LETTER TO REMEMBER

Our friendship and kinship are either childhood friends, college constituents, or sisters for some of you. Then there are the recent ones who have embraced me as their friend. Whether we have longevity or not, I think of the relationship we share.

We have embraced the cold of the winter when we don't hear from each other for months, during which times we have endured such cold, arduous challenges from life. Then there are the times when our lives spring forth and come alive like the springtime.

The challenges begin to loosen like the ground during the spring season, and we get in touch with renewed strength and contact each other more. I think about the summers we've shared engaging in picnics or perhaps visits, maybe memorable social gatherings, and how our hearts beam because we made it through the tests and trials of problems that appeared so blistering cold we never thought we would come through to the climate of having a comforting moment.

Then I have thought about the fall times of our lives when things that were so hard finally fell off like leaves that dried up as if it never happened or as dried leaves sometimes blow away and some things leave a lingering effect.

A sickness that lingers, the loss of a loved one, an untimely misfortune, or just plain dealing with the aging effects of life. As a gospel singer put it in the song "Precious Memories." "How they linger, how they flood our soul, in the stillness of the midnight Jesus whispers—child I will be with you what a comfort to the soul."

This is a joyous time of the year because we can reflect on the four seasons of our lives and how God has been the bridge that has safely brought us across. It is a time to call others and let them know that Jesus is the reason for the season.

A time when we stuff the stockings of our lives within ourselves and snuggle securely in knowing that the New Year will be familiar because we have matured to a place of acceptance. Wrap yourself in His goodness, grind some coffee beans and let the home smell of fresh coffee, put on a pot of hot water for tea or hot chocolate, and sit at HIS feet because you are special, loved, and you are somebody.

Jacqueline Childs

Until You Sleep In My Bed

AUTHOR BIO

Jacqueline Childs Taliaferro

Jacqueline Childs Taliaferro is a cradle Catholic, spirit-filled, installed Minister and Evangelist. Jacqueline has been graced with many gifts and talents; however, God has endowed her with a creative and over-the-edge anointed writing and singing ability. She is a Christ-centered motivational speaker and Life Skills Coach. Countless lives have been blessed, changed, and transformed by her human experience and miracle-filled revelations and testimonies.

Jacqueline has produced a series of prayerful CDs filled with inspirational words to feed the soul, en-lighten the mind, and uplift the heart of the listeners. She has an extensive record of being used by God at speaking engagements, women's conferences, re-treats, and other mediums of ministry that allow her to reach the broken and touch the lives of many throughout many denominations. Revival is always welcome as Jacqueline travels throughout the United States, spreading God's message of hope.

Jacqueline advocates building strong families as she is happily married, a devoted mother, and a grandmother.

Jacqueline Childs Taliaferro's life's motto is found in Isaiah 60:1, "Arise, shine for thy light is come, and the glory of the Lord is risen upon thee."

I appreciate your support, and may God bless you always. For more information about my book and/or if you want to give me feedback, please get in touch with me at jctalia@yahoo.com.

Made in the USA
Middletown, DE
27 September 2022